A QUICK GUIDE

JUDAISM

An easy guide to Judaism, its history,
Jewish beliefs, sacred text, customs and tradition

ALEX RICHARDS

CONTENTS

PREFACE   7

1. INTRODUCTION TO JUDAISM   9
   Defining Judaism   10
   Jewish Beliefs   12
   Why Understanding Judaism in a Global
   Context is Important   14

2. HISTORICAL BACKGROUND OF JUDAISM   17
   Ancient Hebrew Culture and Society   17
   The Patriarchs and Matriarchs   19
   The Exodus from Egypt and the Giving of the
   Torah   22
   The Exodus from Egypt   22
   The Giving of the Torah   25
   King David   26

3. BELIEFS IN JUDAISM   29
   Monotheism in Judaism   29
   The Shema Prayer   30
   The 13 Principles of Faith by Maimonides   31
   The Jewish View of the Messiah   32

4. SACRED TEXTS   36
   The Hebrew Bible (Tanakh)   36
   Torah: The Foundation of Jewish Law and
   Belief   37
   Nevi'im (Prophets): Insights and Prophecies   39
   Latter Prophets   42
   The Talmud: The Oral Torah Preserved   47
   Halakha   49
   Other Important Jewish Texts and
   Commentaries   51

5. PRACTICES AND CUSTOMS   54
   Sabbath (Shabbat) Observance: A Day of Rest
   and Holiness   54
   Dietary Laws (Kashrut) and Kosher Food:
   Spiritual Nutrition   56
   Lifecycle Events: Marking Significant
   Moments   59
   The Mezuzah: A Symbol of Jewish Faith,
   Identity, and Commitment   61
   Synagogue Worship and Prayer Services:
   Communal and Individual Devotion   63

6. PHILOSOPHY AND THEOLOGY:
   EXPLORING THE DEPTHS OF FAITH   67
   Different Jewish Denominations: Varieties of
   Belief and Practice   67
   The Concept of Chosenness and Covenant: A
   Unique Relationship with God   71
   Jewish Ethics and Moral Principles: A
   Blueprint for Righteous Living   73
   Jewish Mysticism (Kabbalah): The Hidden
   Dimensions of Faith   74

7. THE SPREAD OF JUDAISM AND THE
   JEWISH DIASPORA: A GLOBAL JOURNEY   76
   The Jewish Diaspora: A Historical Overview   76
   Influence of Judaism in Various Regions   78
   Challenges and Opportunities of Maintaining
   Jewish Identity in Different Contexts   80

8. CULTURE AND TRADITIONS: A TAPESTRY
   OF HERITAGE   83
   Jewish Art, Music, and Literature: Expressions
   of Identity and Faith   83
   Jewish Music   85
   Jewish Literature   86
   Jewish Festivals and Holidays: Celebrating
   History and Faith   87
   The Importance of Preserving and Passing
   Down Jewish Traditions   89

9. CONTEMPORARY ISSUES: JUDAISM IN
   THE MODERN WORLD   93
   Anti-Semitism   93
   Historical Persecution of Jews   94
   Anti-Semitism in the Modern World   98
   Challenges and Debates within the Jewish
   Community   99
   Assimilation and the Preservation of Jewish
   Identity   100
   Interfaith Relations and Dialogue   102
   The Israeli-Palestinian Conflict   103
   Gender and Religious Leadership   104
   Conversion and Inclusivity   105
   The Role of Judaism in Social Justice and
   Humanitarian Causes   106

10. CONCLUSION   109
11. GLOSSARY   111

    About the Author   117

PREFACE

'A QUICK GUIDE' SERIES

The 'A Quick Guide' series is carefully crafted to provide you with a concise overview of various subjects, enabling you to grasp their core essentials in a quick and easy-to-read format. These books serve as an 'all-you-need-to-know' introduction that can be comfortably read in just a few hours.

We trim away extraneous information to present the essential foundations, so you can build a strong understanding without becoming entangled in unnecessary details.

Whether you're seeking to expand your knowledge or simply curious about a particular subject, our books promise to be enlightening and thought-provoking experiences.

Look out for more titles in the 'A Quick Guide' series, covering historical figures, ancient civilizations, wars, religion, philosophy, and more, available at www.aquickguide-books.com.

1

INTRODUCTION TO JUDAISM

Judaism is one of the world's oldest and most influential religions, deeply rooted in history, culture, and spirituality. With a history that spans over three millennia, it is more than just a religion; it's a comprehensive way of life that has had a profound impact on the world.

In an increasingly interconnected world, a comprehensive understanding of Judaism is not only valuable but also necessary for promoting tolerance, cooperation, and peace among diverse religious and cultural communities.

In this quick guide, we'll explore some key aspects of Judaism to help you better understand this unique and influential religion.

DEFINING JUDAISM

At its core, Judaism is one of the three major monotheistic Abrahamic religions, along with Christianity and Islam, that traces its origins to the covenant between God and the biblical figure Abraham. Jews believe in one God, known as Yahweh or Jehovah, who is all-powerful and compassionate.

Its foundational texts include the Hebrew Bible (the Tanakh), which is composed of three parts: the Torah (the first five books, also known as the Pentateuch), the Prophets, and the Writings. Judaism's primary sacred scripture is the Torah, which encompasses religious laws, ethical teachings, and historical narratives, and its study plays a crucial role in Jewish education and spiritual growth.

Judaism is often described as both a religion and a way of life. This dual nature is reflected in its multifaceted definition.

Religion

Judaism involves the worship of one God, Yahweh, who is seen as the creator of the universe and the source of moral guidance. The Jewish faith is centered on the belief in this unique and all-powerful deity.

Ethnicity and Identity

Jewish identity is not solely defined by religious beliefs; it is also deeply connected to shared history, culture, and traditions. The Jewish people have a unique linguistic heritage with Hebrew, and they celebrate a diverse array of festivals, including Passover, Hanukkah, Rosh Hashanah, and Yom Kippur. These celebrations reflect the rich tapestry of Jewish life.

In Jewish communities, you'll find synagogues, places of worship and communal gatherings. Rabbis, spiritual leaders, guide the congregations in prayer, study, and life events such as weddings and funerals. The synagogue serves as a hub for Jewish life, fostering a sense of togetherness and spiritual growth.

Kosher dietary laws are another distinctive feature of Judaism. These laws dictate which foods are considered permissible and how they should be prepared and consumed. While not all Jews adhere to kosher dietary restrictions, it's a way for many to infuse their daily lives with their faith.

The Star of David, named after King David, is a six-pointed star, and is an iconic symbol of Judaism and Jewish identity and heritage. It represents the unity of the Jewish people and is displayed on the flag of Israel.

Covenantal Relationship

One of the central concepts in Judaism is the covenant, a sacred agreement between God and the Jewish people. This covenant was established with the biblical figure Abraham and is a source of guidance and responsibility. Jews believe that by following God's commandments, or mitzvot, they maintain their end of the covenant and receive God's protection and blessings in return.

Tradition and Heritage

Judaism places a strong emphasis on preserving traditions, rituals, and historical narratives. The preservation of Jewish heritage is a significant part of Jewish identity.

JEWISH BELIEFS

Judaism is characterized by several key beliefs and principles that have shaped the faith and the Jewish people's worldview.

Monotheism

The belief in one God, Yahweh, is the foundational tenet of Judaism. This one God is all-powerful, all-knowing, and compassionate, and is the source of both creation and moral guidance.

The Covenant

The Covenant between God and the Jewish people, as established with Abraham, forms the basis of the relationship between Jews and God. It entails a set of obligations and promises, including the observance of God's commandments (mitzvot) and God's protection and guidance.

Torah

The Torah is the central and holiest text in Judaism. It contains the divine laws, commandments, and narratives that guide Jewish life. Observant Jews study and interpret the Torah to understand God's will and how to live a righteous life.

The Importance of Deeds

Judaism places a strong emphasis on good deeds and ethical behavior. Acts of kindness, charity, and justice are integral to the Jewish way of life, and are encouraged to engage in these acts to strengthen their connection with God and to promote a just and compassionate world.

Messianic Hope

Most Jews (with the exception of a few groups) believe that their Messiah (Mashiach) has yet to come, to restore peace, justice, and righteousness to the world. The concept of the Messiah varies among different Jewish denominations.

Afterlife

Beliefs about the afterlife in Judaism are diverse. While some Jewish traditions believe in a form of an afterlife, others emphasize the importance of living a righteous life in the present rather than focusing on what may come after death.

WHY UNDERSTANDING JUDAISM IN A GLOBAL CONTEXT IS IMPORTANT

Understanding Judaism is vital in a global context for several reasons.

Interfaith Dialogue

In an increasingly interconnected world, promoting understanding and tolerance among different faith communities is essential. A comprehensive understanding of Judaism enables more effective interfaith dialogue and cooperation, which can lead to greater social cohesion and peace.

Historical Significance

Judaism is the foundation of both Christianity and Islam, two of the world's most widespread religions. Knowledge of Judaism's history and beliefs helps us understand the historical context in which these religions emerged and the shared elements of the Abrahamic tradition.

Cultural and Ethical Influence

Jewish culture and ethics have had a profound impact on various aspects of global society, including literature, art, philosophy, and ethics. A deeper understanding of Judaism helps us appreciate the contributions of Jewish individuals and communities to the world.

Contemporary Issues

Understanding Judaism is critical when addressing contemporary issues related to anti-Semitism, the Israeli-Palestinian conflict, and religious pluralism. Knowledge about Judaism helps promote informed discussions and problem-solving.

Multifaceted Identity

Judaism's dual nature as a religion and an ethnic identity makes it an intriguing case study in the complexities of human identity. This dual identity has implications for global discussions on multiculturalism, diversity, and belonging.

Religious Freedom and Human Rights

An understanding of Judaism is crucial for advancing principles of religious freedom and human rights worldwide. By appreciating the struggles and achievements of Jewish communities, we can better advocate for these rights globally.

DID YOU KNOW?

When praying, Jews turn towards the Temple Mount, the holiest site for Jews. However, since it's forbidden to pray there, due to its sacredness, The Western Wall (also known as the Wailing Wall) in Jerusalem is the holiest site for prayer and pilgrimage.

Located in the Old City of Jerusalem, The Western is a remnant of the retaining wall that surrounded the Second

Temple, which was destroyed by the Romans in 70 CE. It has become a place of deep religious significance and visitors leave written prayers, called kvitlach or notes, in the crevices of the wall.

Source:
https://www.havefunwithhistory.com/facts-about-judaism/

2

HISTORICAL BACKGROUND OF JUDAISM

To understand Judaism, we need to explore its historical roots, the ancient Hebrew culture and society in which it developed, and the pivotal figures and events that shaped the faith including the Exodus from Egypt, and the giving of the Torah.

ANCIENT HEBREW CULTURE AND SOCIETY

Let's step back in time to ancient Canaan, a region in the eastern Mediterranean. The people who would become the Hebrews were part of this diverse and culturally rich area. The ancient Hebrews were pastoralists and agriculturalists, and their society was organized around family clans and tribes.

Family and Clan
Ancient Hebrew society placed a strong emphasis on family and kinship ties. Families were the basic social units, and clans, which were larger groups of related families, formed the basis of community life. Loyalty to one's clan and tribe was crucial.

Religion
Religion was an integral part of daily life for the ancient Hebrews. They believed in a pantheon of deities, with El (the chief god) and Asherah (the mother goddess) being prominent. Over time, their religious beliefs evolved towards monotheism, culminating in the worship of the one God, Yahweh.

Language
The Hebrew language, a Semitic language (which includes Arabic, Aramaic and Amharic), played a central role in shaping Hebrew identity. It became the vehicle for their sacred texts, prayers, and cultural expressions.

Covenant and Ethics
Even in ancient times, the Hebrews held a strong sense of moral and ethical values. This would later become a cornerstone of Judaism. The notion of a covenant between God and the people, a binding agreement, started to take root.

THE PATRIARCHS AND MATRIARCHS

The foundational figures of Judaism, known as the patriarchs and matriarchs, are at the heart of its history. These individuals are considered the ancestors of the Jewish people and played pivotal roles in the development of the faith. Their stories are commemorated and celebrated throughout the Jewish calendar.

Patriarchs

Abraham (Abram)
Abraham is often referred to as the "Father of Monotheism." He is considered the first patriarch and is known for his unwavering faith in one God, Yahweh. According to the Hebrew Bible, God made a covenant with Abraham, promising him numerous descendants and the land of Canaan (the Promised Land). Abraham's obedience to God's command to circumcise himself and his male descendants symbolizes his commitment to the covenant.

Isaac
Isaac, the son of Abraham and Sarah, is the second patriarch. His birth was miraculous, as it occurred in their old age. Isaac is a central figure in the biblical narrative, as he was bound by his father for sacrifice in the story of the Akedah (the Binding of Isaac). This event is a symbol of obedience to God's will.

Jacob (Israel)

Jacob, also known as Israel, is the third patriarch. He had twelve sons, each of whom became the ancestor of one of the twelve tribes of Israel. His transformation from a cunning individual to a man of faith and character is a significant theme in the Hebrew Bible.

The division of the Israelite people into these twelve (or thirteen) tribes is a fundamental aspect of their identity and history. Each tribe had its own characteristics, territory, and responsibilities, and they often united or formed alliances during times of war or national crises.

Matriarchs

Sarah

Sarah, the wife of Abraham, is considered the first matriarch. Her story includes her laughter upon hearing that she would have a son in her old age, which led to the naming of their son, Isaac. Sarah is known for her beauty and her role in the biblical narrative as the mother of the Israelite nation.

Rebekah

Rebekah is the wife of Isaac and the mother of Jacob and Esau. She played a central role in securing the birthright and blessing for Jacob, despite her husband Isaac's initial preference for Esau.

Rachel and Leah

Rachel and Leah were sisters and wives of Jacob. They are both considered matriarchs and are known for their role in the complex story of Jacob's marriages, as well as for bearing many of Jacob's sons. Rachel is especially known for her beauty, and her son, Joseph, played a significant role in the biblical narrative.

Let's look at the important functions played by these Patriarchs and Matriarchs.

Ancestral Foundations

They are seen as the progenitors of the Jewish people, and their descendants are often referred to as the "Children of Israel."

Covenant Bearers

The Patriarchs, particularly Abraham, are associated with the establishment of the covenant between God and the Israelites. They serve as examples of faith and obedience.

Role Models

The lives and experiences of the Patriarchs and Matriarchs offer moral and ethical lessons, as well as examples of resilience, faith, and devotion to God.

Symbols of Jewish Identity

The stories of these figures are foundational to Jewish identity and are retold in various forms, including in Jewish literature, art, and religious practice.

THE EXODUS FROM EGYPT AND THE GIVING OF THE TORAH

One of the most important and celebrated events in Jewish history is the Exodus from Egypt, which marks the deliverance of the Hebrews from slavery and their journey to the Promised Land.

THE EXODUS FROM EGYPT

The story of the Exodus is primarily recounted in the Book of Exodus in the Hebrew Bible. It is the story of the Israelites' liberation from slavery in Egypt and their journey to freedom and the Promised Land.

The Israelite Slavery

The story begins with the Israelites living in Egypt under the oppressive rule of Pharaoh, who orders the enslavement of the Israelite population. This period of bondage represents the initial hardship endured by the Israelites.

Birth and Calling of Moses

Moses, one of the most prominent figures in the Hebrew Bible, is born during this time. He is selected by God to be the leader and prophet who will guide the Israelites out of

Egypt. Moses' calling, symbolized by the burning bush, is a pivotal moment in the story.

God's Ten Plagues

In response to Pharaoh's refusal to free the Israelite slaves, God inflicts ten devastating plagues upon Egypt. These plagues include water turning to blood, frogs, lice, wild animals, pestilence, boils, hail, locusts, darkness, and the death of the firstborn. The final plague, the death of the first-born, leads Pharaoh to relent and allow the Israelites to leave.

The Passover

The Israelites celebrate the Passover as a commemoration of their protection during the final plague. They mark their doorposts with lamb's blood so that the angel of death would "pass over" their households, sparing their firstborn.

The Exodus

Following the Passover, the Israelites depart from Egypt, a mass departure known as the Exodus. They leave in haste, taking with them unleavened bread (matzah) as they have no time to let their bread dough rise. This unleavened bread becomes an essential element of the Passover celebration.

The Parting of the Red Sea

As the Israelites flee, they are pursued by Pharaoh's army. Miraculously, God parts the Red Sea, allowing the Israelites to cross on dry land. However, when the Egyptian army attempts to follow, the waters close in on them, drowning Pharaoh's forces.

Journey through the Wilderness
The Israelites continue their journey, facing various challenges and receiving divine guidance, such as the provision of manna (heavenly food) and water from a rock.

The Exodus holds immense importance in Judaism:

Identity
It serves as a foundational narrative, symbolizing the Jewish people's liberation from oppression and their unique identity as a chosen people.

Covenant with God
The Exodus marked the beginning of the covenant between God and the Israelites. At Mount Sinai, the Israelites received the Torah, the divine law, and a set of ethical and religious principles that have guided Jewish life for millennia.

Ethical Imperative
The memory of their own suffering as slaves in Egypt instills in Jewish tradition a strong ethical imperative to work for justice, protect the vulnerable, and combat oppression.

Passover
The Passover holiday commemorates the Exodus and is one

of the most widely celebrated Jewish festivals. It includes the retelling of the story, the Seder meal, and the consumption of unleavened bread, or matzah.

THE GIVING OF THE TORAH

The Giving of the Torah occurred at Mount Sinai after the Israelites had left Egypt. According to the biblical account, God revealed the Torah to Moses and the Israelites in a theophanic event, marked by thunder, lightning, and the sounding of a shofar (a ram's horn). The Torah consists of the first five books of the Hebrew Bible, including the Ten Commandments and a comprehensive set of laws and teachings.

The Giving of the Torah is of paramount significance in Judaism for several reasons.

Divine Revelation
It represents the idea of direct divine revelation, where God communicated the ethical and religious laws to humanity. This moment is seen as a unique and unrepeatable event in history.

Ethical and Moral Code
The Torah contains the ethical and moral code by which Jews are to live their lives. The Ten Commandments, in particular, provide the foundational principles for Jewish ethics.

Legal Framework

The Torah includes the legal and ritual framework that governs all aspects of Jewish life, from dietary laws (kashrut) to family and communal responsibilities.

Covenant Renewal

The giving of the Torah is a reaffirmation of the covenant established with the patriarchs and is seen as the binding agreement between God and the Jewish people.

KING DAVID

King David's legacy is a central and revered figure in Judaism, known for his role in the Bible, particularly in the Hebrew Scriptures or Tanakh. He is often referred to as the "sweet singer of Israel" due to his poetic contributions in the Psalms, and his story is a source of inspiration for concepts such as repentance, divine covenant, and the messianic hope.

The Davidic dynasty is a significant theme in Jewish messianic expectations, with the belief that the ultimate Messiah (Mashiach) will be a descendant of King David, fulfilling the promises made in the Davidic Covenant.

David is considered one of the greatest kings of ancient Israel and is associated with various significant events and accomplishments.

Anointed King by the Prophet Samuel

According to the biblical narrative, David was anointed as

king by the prophet Samuel while Saul was still the reigning king. This event is seen as God's choice of David to be the future ruler of Israel.

Defeating Goliath
One of the most famous stories about David is his victory over the Philistine giant, Goliath. Despite being a young shepherd, David's faith in God and his skill with a sling allowed him to defeat Goliath and became a symbol of triumph against seemingly insurmountable odds.

Friendship with Jonathan
David's close friendship with Jonathan, the son of King Saul, is highlighted in the biblical narrative. Their friendship is often cited as an example of loyalty and devotion.

Establishing Jerusalem as the Capital
King David is credited with establishing Jerusalem as the capital of the United Kingdom of Israel. He captured the city from the Jebusites and made it a central religious and political center.

The Davidic Covenant
In 2 Samuel 7, there is an account of the Davidic Covenant, where God promises David that his descendants will establish an enduring kingdom. This covenant is significant in Jewish theology as it is believed to be the basis for the messianic expectations associated with the line of David.

Composer of Psalms

King David is traditionally credited with composing many of the Psalms found in the Book of Psalms (Tehillim). These hymns and prayers are an integral part of Jewish worship and are recited in various religious contexts.

Flaws and Repentance

The biblical narrative also presents the flaws and challenges in David's life, including his affair with Bathsheba and the subsequent murder of her husband Uriah. Despite these transgressions, David is praised for his sincere repentance and acknowledgment of wrongdoing.

Death and Succession

David's reign is described as a time of military success and political consolidation. He ruled for 40 years and was succeeded by his son Solomon.

DID YOU KNOW?

The term "Semitic" is derived from "Shem," one of the sons of Noah in the Bible. According to the Book of Genesis in the Hebrew Bible, Noah had three sons: Shem, Ham, and Japheth. Shem is traditionally considered the ancestor of the Semitic peoples, and his descendants are believed to have given rise to various Semitic-speaking cultures and civilizations.

3

BELIEFS IN JUDAISM

J udaism is defined by a set of core beliefs and principles that underpin the faith, practice, and identity of Jewish people. These beliefs have shaped the essence of Judaism for millennia, reflecting the faith's enduring and profound impact on both individuals and the broader global context.

MONOTHEISM IN JUDAISM

The concept of monotheism is the cornerstone of Judaism. At its core, monotheism is the belief in the existence of a single, transcendent, and all-powerful God. In the case of Judaism, this God is known by various names, with "Yahweh" and "Jehovah" being two of the most common. This singular divine entity is both immanent and transcendent, meaning that God is present in the world and yet beyond it.

Monotheism is not just an abstract theological concept in Judaism; it is a foundational belief that permeates every aspect of Jewish life. The idea of one God is encapsulated in the Shema, a central declaration of faith in Judaism.

THE SHEMA PRAYER

The Shema is one of the most significant and widely recognized prayers in Judaism, found in the Torah (Deuteronomy 6:4-9). Its central declaration is:

"Hear, O Israel: The LORD our God, the LORD is one. Love the LORD your God with all your heart and with all your soul and with all your strength."

This proclamation encapsulates the essence of monotheism and serves as a daily affirmation of Jewish belief in the one true God. The Shema emphasizes not only the oneness of God but also the call to love and serve God with unwavering devotion.

In Jewish tradition, the Shema is recited in morning and evening prayers, as well as before bedtime, and is often the first prayer taught to Jewish children. It is a reminder of the Jewish commitment to monotheism and the love and loyalty owed to God. The Shema represents more than a theological statement; it is a way to connect with God on a deeply personal and spiritual level.

Maimonides, also known as Rambam (Rabbi Moses ben Maimon), was a renowned Jewish philosopher, scholar, and physician who lived in the 12th century. He is best known for his work "The Thirteen Principles of Faith," a comprehensive articulation of the core beliefs in Judaism. Maimonides' principles offer a systematic and rationalized approach to understanding Jewish faith, and they continue to hold a prominent place in Jewish thought and practice.

The 13 Principles of Faith by Maimonides are as follows:

1. Belief in the existence of God: This is the foundational principle, acknowledging the one true God.
2. God's unity and incorporeality: God is indivisible and lacks physical form.
3. God's eternity: God has always existed and will continue to exist eternally.
4. God alone should be the object of worship: Worship is to be directed solely to God and not to any other beings.
5. Belief in the existence of prophecy: Judaism recognizes the legitimacy of prophets as a means of divine communication.
6. Belief in the authenticity of the prophetic nature of Moses: Moses is considered the greatest prophet and the mediator of the Torah.

7. Belief in the divine origin of the Torah: The Torah is believed to be of divine origin and is the foundational text of Judaism.
8. Belief in the immutability of the Torah: The Torah is unchanging and continues to be binding.
9. Belief in God's omniscience: God is all-knowing and has perfect knowledge of all things.
10. Belief in divine reward and punishment: God rewards the righteous and punishes the wicked.
11. Belief in the coming of the Messiah: The Messiah is expected to bring about the redemption of the Jewish people and the establishment of peace and justice.
12. Belief in the resurrection of the dead: The dead will be resurrected in the messianic era.
13. Belief in the final judgment: There will be a final judgment of all human beings by God.

Maimonides' 13 Principles provide a systematic framework for Jewish theology and a guide for Jewish belief. While not all Jewish denominations adhere to these principles with equal emphasis, they represent a key statement of faith that continues to shape Jewish thought and practice to this day.

THE JEWISH VIEW OF THE MESSIAH

The Jewish view of the Messiah, often referred to as the "Mashiach" in Hebrew, is a fundamental component of

Jewish eschatology (the part of theology dealing with death, judgement and the final destination of the soul) and belief. However, it differs significantly from the Christian concept of the Messiah. In Judaism, the Messiah is envisioned as a human leader, not divine, who will play a specific role in the redemption of the Jewish people and the establishment of a utopian era marked by peace, justice, and the recognition of God's sovereignty.

Key elements of the Jewish view of the Messiah include:

Human Leader
The Messiah is expected to be a human being, a descendant of King David, who will fulfill specific prophecies outlined in the Hebrew Bible.

Redemption of the Jewish People
The Messiah's primary role is to lead the Jewish people out of exile and gather them back to the land of Israel.

Rebuilding of the Temple
The Messiah is anticipated to oversee the rebuilding of the Holy Temple in Jerusalem.

World Peace and Recognition of God
Under the Messiah's leadership, there will be a universal recognition of God's sovereignty, and the world will experience an era of unprecedented peace and justice.

It is important to note that the Jewish concept of the Messiah is not associated with divine nature or having a role leading to salvation, as it is in Christianity. Instead, the Messiah is seen as a pivotal human figure who will bring about a messianic age and fulfill specific prophetic expectations.

In summary, the four central beliefs in Judaism - monotheism, the Shema prayer, Maimonides' 13 Principles of Faith, and the Jewish view of the Messiah - provide a comprehensive understanding of Jewish faith, theology, and the enduring connection between Jewish belief and practice. These beliefs have been foundational to Jewish identity for centuries and continue to shape the spiritual, ethical, and cultural dimensions of Jewish life.

DID YOU KNOW?

Jewish identity is passed down matrilineally, meaning that a person is considered Jewish if their mother is Jewish. This principle, known as "Jewish descent through the mother," has been a longstanding tradition in Jewish law.

However, various Jewish movements have different approaches to this concept, with some recognizing patrilineal descent as well. Conversion to Judaism is another pathway to Jewish identity, involving a process of study, acceptance of Jewish beliefs and practices, and immersion in a ritual bath called a mikveh.

Source:

https://www.havefunwithhistory.com/facts-about-judaism/

4

SACRED TEXTS

Judaism possesses a vast and diverse collection of sacred texts spanning thousands of years. These texts are the foundation of Jewish faith, practice, and identity. Let's delve into some of the most important Jewish sacred texts, including the Hebrew Bible (Tanakh), the Talmud, and other vital texts and commentaries, such as Midrash, that play integral roles in Jewish law, theology, and tradition.

THE HEBREW BIBLE (TANAKH)

At the heart of Jewish sacred literature lies the Hebrew Bible, known as the "Tanakh." The Tanakh is an acronym derived from its three primary divisions: Torah, Nevi'im (Prophets), and Ketuvim (Writings). Each section of the Tanakh holds a unique significance within Jewish tradition.

TORAH: THE FOUNDATION OF JEWISH LAW AND BELIEF

The Torah, meaning "teaching" or "instruction," is the most revered and central component of the Tanakh. It consists of the first five books of the Bible: Genesis (Bereshit), Exodus (Shemot), Leviticus (Vayikra), Numbers (Bemidbar), and Deuteronomy (Devarim). These books encompass a wide range of narratives, laws, commandments, and moral teachings.

Genesis (Bereshit) – The Story of Creation and Early History

The Book of Genesis, the opening act of the Bible, is a captivating journey through the dawn of creation. It's a tale of beginnings, where God's creative genius springs forth, shaping the heavens, the earth, and all living creatures.

From the formation of Adam and Eve in the Garden of Eden to the iconic story of Noah's Ark, and the patriarchs and matriarchs, including Abraham, Isaac, Jacob, and Joseph, and Genesis offers vivid accounts of humanity's earliest chapters and the covenant between God and His chosen people.

Exodus (Shemot) and the Covenant

Exodus is a pivotal narrative chronicling the liberation of the Israelites from slavery in Egypt. It unfolds the story of Moses, God's chosen leader, and the ten plagues that compelled Pharaoh to release the Israelites. The book details their escape, the parting of the Red Sea, and their journey to Mount Sinai, where they receive the Ten Commandments.

Exodus signifies the fulfillment of God's promise to Abraham, the establishment of the covenant between God and the Jewish people and the birth of the Israelite nation.

Leviticus (Vayikra) and Numbers (Bamidbar) – A Legal Code

Leviticus primarily deals with laws and rituals governing religious and moral conduct among the Israelites. It addresses various aspects of life, including dietary rules, offerings, purification rituals, and regulations for priests. The book lays out instructions for atonement, cleanliness, and ethical behavior, emphasizing holiness and the sacred relationship between God and His people. While it may appear legalistic, Leviticus reflects the ancient Israelites' dedication to living in accordance with divine mandates.

Numbers continues the Israelites' journey from Mount Sinai toward the Promised Land. It's named for the censuses and numerical data within its pages. The book includes events such as the sending of spies into Canaan, the Israelites' rebellion, and God's guidance through a pillar of cloud and fire.

Numbers emphasizes themes of divine guidance, trust, and the consequences of disobedience, providing valuable insight into the Israelites' experiences in the wilderness.

Deuteronomy (Devarim) - Moses' Farewell

Deuteronomy is essentially Moses' farewell address to the Israelites. Its name, which means "second law," stems from the way it restates and expands upon the moral and legal instructions found in earlier books. Moses reviews the nation's history, emphasizing the importance of obeying God's commandments in the Promised Land.

Deuteronomy also contains the Shema, a central Jewish declaration of faith calling for wholehearted love and obedience to God. The book underscores themes of covenant, faithfulness, and the enduring relationship between God and His people.

The Torah is regarded as the divine instruction given to the Jewish people by God through the prophet Moses. It serves as the foundation of Jewish law (Halakha), guiding virtually every aspect of Jewish life, from religious observance and moral conduct to dietary regulations and the understanding of God.

NEVI'IM (PROPHETS): INSIGHTS AND PROPHECIES

The Former Prophets, a section of the Nevi'im (Prophets) in the Hebrew Bible, consists of four books: Joshua, Judges, Samuel (comprising 1 Samuel and 2 Samuel), and Kings (comprising 1 Kings and 2 Kings). These books trace the history of the Israelites from their conquest of Canaan under Joshua to the Babylonian exile.

The Former Prophets provide a historical and theological narrative of the Israelites' journey, emphasizing themes of obedience, covenant, leadership, and the consequences of straying from God's commands.

1. Joshua

- Conquest of Canaan: Joshua, Moses' successor, leads the Israelites across the Jordan River and into the Promised Land.
- Jericho: The miraculous fall of the city of Jericho is a key event in the conquest.
- Division of the Land: The land is divided among the tribes of Israel.
- Covenant Renewal: Joshua renews the covenant between God and the people before his death.

2. Judges

- Cycle of Apostasy: The book of Judges describes a cyclical pattern of the Israelites turning away from God, facing oppression by foreign nations, crying out for deliverance, and being rescued by judges.
- Prominent Judges: The book highlights key judges like Deborah, Gideon, Jephthah, and Samson.

- Moral and Spiritual Decline: The stories illustrate the moral and spiritual decline of the Israelites during this period.

3. Samuel

- Samuel's Birth and Calling: The prophet Samuel is born to Hannah and is dedicated to serving God from a young age.
- Transition to Monarchy: The people request a king, and Saul is anointed as the first king of Israel. However, Saul's disobedience leads to God rejecting him as king.
- David's Anointing: David, a shepherd, is anointed as the future king of Israel by the prophet Samuel.
- Saul and David's Relationship: The complex relationship between Saul and David, including David's victory over Goliath and Saul's attempts to kill David.
- David's Reign Begins: David becomes king after Saul's death, uniting the tribes and establishing Jerusalem as the capital.

4. Kings

- Solomon's Reign: Solomon, David's son, builds the Temple in Jerusalem, displaying great wisdom. However, his later years are marked by idolatry and oppression, leading to the division of the kingdom.

- Division of the Kingdom: The Northern Kingdom (Israel) and the Southern Kingdom (Judah) emerge after Solomon's death.
- Prophets and Kings: Various prophets, including Elijah and Elisha, interact with the kings, condemning idolatry and calling for repentance.
- Fall of Israel and Judah: Both kingdoms face the consequences of disobedience, with Israel falling to the Assyrians and Judah to the Babylonians.
- Exile and Hope: The books conclude with the Babylonian exile but also hint at the hope of restoration and a future Messiah.

LATTER PROPHETS

This group comprises major and minor prophets, and includes the books of Isaiah, Jeremiah, Ezekiel, and the Twelve Minor Prophets (Hosea to Malachi). These prophetic books contain a mixture of oracles, visions, and narratives.

The Latter Prophets collectively convey a message of God's justice, mercy, and faithfulness. They address the consequences of disobedience, the promise of restoration, and the anticipation of a future Messiah.

1. Isaiah

- Prophecies of Judgment and Restoration: Isaiah's prophecies include warnings of impending judgment on Israel and other nations due to disobedience, as well as promises of future restoration.

- The Suffering Servant: Notable is the portrayal of the "Suffering Servant," interpreted by Christians as a messianic figure, emphasizing the themes of redemption and atonement.
- Vision of God's Glory: Isaiah experiences a vision of God's glory in the Temple, which serves as a call to prophetic ministry.

2. Jeremiah

- The Weeping Prophet: Jeremiah is known as the "Weeping Prophet" due to his sorrow over the impending destruction of Jerusalem and the exile of the people.
- The New Covenant: Jeremiah prophesies about a new covenant that God will make with His people, written on their hearts, emphasizing a spiritual transformation.
- Persecution and Imprisonment: Jeremiah faces opposition, persecution, and imprisonment for his unpopular messages.

3. Ezekiel

- Visions of God's Glory: Ezekiel experiences vivid visions of God's glory, including the famous vision of the valley of dry bones, symbolizing the restoration of Israel.

- Symbolic Actions: The prophet engages in various symbolic actions, such as lying on his side and eating a scroll, to convey God's messages.
- Prophecies Against Foreign Nations: Ezekiel delivers prophecies of judgment against foreign nations, illustrating God's sovereignty over all nations.

4. The Twelve Minor Prophets (Hosea to Malachi)

- Hosea: Hosea's personal life serves as a metaphor for Israel's unfaithfulness to God. The prophet marries Gomer, who represents Israel's unfaithfulness, yet Hosea remains faithful.
- Joel: Joel speaks of a day of the Lord, emphasizing repentance and restoration.
- Amos: Amos condemns social injustice and calls for repentance, proclaiming that true worship requires righteousness.
- Obadiah: Obadiah declares God's judgment on Edom for their mistreatment of Israel.
- Jonah: Jonah is famously swallowed by a great fish after attempting to evade God's call to prophesy to Nineveh. His story highlights God's mercy even on repentant gentiles.
- Micah: Micah condemns corruption and oppression and foretells the birth of the Messiah in Bethlehem.

- Nahum: Nahum prophesies the downfall of Nineveh, emphasizing God's justice.
- Habakkuk: Habakkuk questions God about the apparent injustice in the world and receives a response about the role of faith.
- Zephaniah: Zephaniah warns of the day of the Lord's judgment but also speaks of future restoration.
- Haggai: Haggai encourages the rebuilding of the Temple after the Babylonian exile, emphasizing God's presence.
- Zechariah: Zechariah envisions the restoration of Jerusalem and the coming of a humble king riding on a donkey.
- Malachi: Malachi addresses issues of social and religious corruption, calling for repentance and announcing the coming of Elijah before the great and dreadful day of the Lord.

3. Ketuvim (Writings): A Diverse Collection of Texts

The Ketuvim, meaning "Writings," is the third section of the Tanakh and consists of a diverse collection of texts. It includes poetry, wisdom literature, historical accounts, and religious songs.

Psalms (Tehillim)
A collection of religious songs and poetry that are central to Jewish liturgy and devotion.

Proverbs (Mishlei)
A compilation of wise sayings and ethical teachings, attributed primarily to King Solomon.

Job (Iyov)
A profound exploration of human suffering and theodicy, addressing questions about the nature of God and the existence of evil.

Song of Songs (Shir HaShirim)
An allegorical love poem that is both an expression of human love and an allegory of the love between God and Israel.

Ruth (Rut)
A narrative about loyalty, faith, and the genealogy of King David.

Lamentations (Eicha)
A collection of five poems that mourn the destruction of the First Temple and the suffering of the Jewish people.

Ecclesiastes (Kohelet)
A philosophical exploration of the meaning of life, wisdom, and the nature of existence.

Esther (Ester)
A narrative of the Jewish heroine Esther, who saves her people from annihilation in Persia.

Daniel (Daniel)
A collection of stories and apocalyptic visions set in the Babylonian exile.

The Ketuvim encompasses a wide range of literary genres and themes, offering insights into the human experience, religious devotion, and the relationship between God and humanity.

THE TALMUD: THE ORAL TORAH PRESERVED

While the Tanakh forms the written foundation of Jewish sacred texts, it is a key component of the Oral Torah. The Talmud is a vast and intricate compilation of rabbinic discussions, commentaries, interpretations, and legal teachings, and it is central to Jewish law and tradition.

The Talmud is divided into two primary components:

1. Mishnah

The Mishnah is a concise and systematic compilation of Jewish laws and traditions, attributed primarily to Rabbi Judah the Prince (Rabbi Yehuda HaNasi) in the 2nd century CE. It is organized into six major divisions, or "orders," each covering different areas of Jewish life, such as prayer, festivals, dietary laws, and civil law.

2. Gemara

The Gemara is a vast and detailed commentary on the Mishnah. It is the product of centuries of rabbinic discussions and interpretations of the Mishnah. The two primary versions of the Gemara are the Babylonian Talmud and the Jerusalem Talmud, with the Babylonian Talmud being more widely studied and recognized.

The Talmud serves multiple functions in Jewish tradition:

Legal Interpretation
It provides detailed explanations and interpretations of the laws and commandments found in the Torah and Mishnah.

Ethical and Philosophical Exploration
The Talmud engages in philosophical discussions, moral reflections, and theological inquiries.

Preservation of Oral Tradition
It safeguards the oral teachings and traditions that were passed down through generations of rabbis.

Foundation of Jewish Law
The Talmud forms the basis for Halakha, the Jewish legal system, and is instrumental in shaping Jewish observance and customs.

The Talmud is a dynamic and living text, constantly studied and interpreted by scholars, rabbis, and Jewish communities worldwide. It is an intellectual and spiritual treasure trove that continues to inform Jewish life and thought.

HALAKHA

Halakha, often spelled as "halacha" or "halachah," is the body of Jewish religious law and tradition that evolved since biblical times to regulate religious observances and the daily life and conduct of the Jewish people.

The term "halakha" is derived from the Hebrew root "halakh," which means "to walk" or "to go." In this context, it signifies the "path" or "way" that Jewish individuals are expected to follow in their lives in accordance with Jewish law and ethical principles. Halakha serves as the practical guide for how Jews should live, worship, and conduct themselves in their daily activities.

Key aspects of Halakha include:

Source
The primary source of Halakha is the Torah, specifically the first five books, which include the commandments and laws given by God to Moses. These texts provide the foundational principles upon which the entire system of Jewish law is built and the Halakha explains the practical application of the 613 mitzvot ("commandments") in the Torah.

Oral Law
In addition to the written Torah, the Oral Law, known as the

"Oral Torah" or "Oral Tradition," plays a critical role in the development of Halakha. According to Jewish tradition, alongside the written Torah, God also provided Moses with oral explanations and interpretations of the laws. These oral teachings were passed down through generations by word of mouth until they were eventually compiled in written form as the Mishnah.

Mishnah and Talmud
The Mishnah is the first written compilation of the Oral Law, attributed to Rabbi Judah the Prince in the 2nd century CE. The Talmud, which includes the Mishnah and extensive rabbinic commentary, further expands and clarifies Halakha. The Talmud is central to the development and understanding of Jewish law.

Legal Codes
Over the centuries, numerous legal codes have been developed to organize and interpret the vast body of Halakha. Prominent among these are the Mishneh Torah by Maimonides and the Shulchan Aruch. These codes help individuals and communities apply Halakha to their lives.

Rabbinic Authority
Rabbis, as religious scholars and authorities, play a pivotal role in interpreting and applying Halakha. Their expertise is essential in addressing complex legal and ethical issues.

Scope

Halakha is not limited to ritual or religious matters. It covers a wide range of topics, including dietary laws (kashrut), Sabbath observance (Shabbat), family life (marriage, divorce, and family purity), business ethics, social justice, and more. It guides every aspect of a Jewish person's life.

Flexibility and Adaptation

While Halakha is rooted in ancient texts and traditions, it has shown an ability to adapt and evolve over time. Jewish legal scholars have developed mechanisms for addressing new situations and dilemmas that arise in a changing world. This adaptability has allowed Halakha to remain relevant in the modern era.

OTHER IMPORTANT JEWISH TEXTS AND COMMENTARIES

In addition to the Tanakh, the Talmud, and the Mishnah, Jewish tradition features a rich array of texts and commentaries that contribute to the depth and breadth of Jewish learning. Among these, one of the most significant categories is Midrash.

Midrash

Midrash (meaning 'to inquire') is a collection of rabbinic commentaries, exegeses, and homiletical interpretations of the Hebrew Bible. It delves into the hidden meanings, ethical lessons, and moral insights found within the biblical texts.

Midrashim (plural of Midrash) often take the form of imaginative stories, parables, and allegories to illuminate the text's deeper significance. Midrash can be halakhic, focusing on legal interpretations, or aggadic, dealing with moral and ethical teachings.

There are four principal methods of midrashic interpretation:

- Peshat: the 'plain' or 'literal' sense of a passage.
- Remez: meaning 'hint' or allusive meaning.
- Derash: the homiletical meaning.
- Sod: the hidden, mystical meaning.

Together these four terms form the acronym PaRDeS.

Some well-known Midrashic collections include the Midrash Rabbah, Midrash Tanchuma, and the Mechilta. Midrash plays a crucial role in both the study of the Torah and the development of Jewish theology and ethics.

These sacred texts and commentaries, along with numerous others not mentioned here, collectively contribute to the rich tapestry of Jewish literature and thought. They inform Jewish law, ethics, theology, and the vibrant traditions that have been handed down through generations, ensuring the continuity of Jewish faith and identity.

DID YOU KNOW?

There are around 15.7 million Jews worldwide making Judaism the 10th largest religion in the world. 46% live in Israel and the United States has the second-largest Jewish population with around 6.3 million.

27,000 Jews live in Muslim-majority countries, with 14,200 in Turkey, 9,100 in Iran, 2,100 in Morocco, 1,000 in Tunisia, and 500 in the United Arab Emirates.

80 countries have Jewish populations between 100 and 10,000 people.

India has a diverse and ancient Jewish community, including Bene Israel, Baghdadi Jews, and Cochin Jews. They have lived in India for generations and have unique customs and traditions.

The Kaifeng Jews have a long history in China, dating back to the Tang Dynasty (7th-10th centuries).

Source:
https://www.timesofisrael.com/global-jewish-population-hits-15-7-million-ahead-of-new-year-46-of-them-in-israel

5

PRACTICES AND CUSTOMS

J udaism is rich in tradition, rituals, and customs that reflect the faith's deep connection to God and its enduring commitment to ethical living. These customs not only define Jewish identity but also provide a roadmap for leading a life of holiness, purpose, and connection with the divine.

SABBATH (SHABBAT) OBSERVANCE: A DAY OF REST AND HOLINESS

Shabbat, often referred to as the "Jewish Sabbath," is one of the most cherished and widely observed Jewish customs. It is a day of rest and spiritual rejuvenation, lasting from Friday evening at sunset to Saturday evening when the first three stars appear in the sky. Shabbat commemorates the biblical account of God's creation of the world in six days, with the seventh day set apart as a day of rest and holiness.

Key elements of Shabbat observance include:

Candle Lighting
Shabbat begins with the lighting of candles by Jewish women, ushering in a sense of peace and sanctity.

Kiddush
The Kiddush, a blessing over wine or grape juice, is recited to sanctify the Sabbath. A special challah (braided bread) is also blessed.

Rest and Abstention
Observant Jews refrain from engaging in work, commerce, writing, and the use of electronic devices during Shabbat. It is a day of rest and spiritual reflection.

Synagogue Services
Attending synagogue services on Friday evening and Saturday morning is a central aspect of Shabbat observance, where special prayers and readings are offered.

Family Meals
The Friday night and Saturday afternoon meals are times for gathering with family and friends to enjoy festive and spiritually uplifting meals. The bread is typically covered by a

challah cover, and blessings are recited over wine or grape juice.

Havdalah

At the conclusion of Shabbat on Saturday evening, a special ceremony called Havdalah is performed, marking the separation between the sacred time of Shabbat and the ordinary workweek. A braided candle, wine or grape juice, and spices are used in this ritual.

Shabbat serves as a weekly opportunity to rest, recharge, connect with loved ones, and deepen one's relationship with God. It is a time of joy, reflection, and celebration of the sanctity of time itself.

DIETARY LAWS (KASHRUT) AND KOSHER FOOD: SPIRITUAL NUTRITION

Kashrut, the system of dietary laws in Judaism, regulates what foods are permissible for consumption. Observing kashrut involves adherence to specific dietary rules and the consumption of kosher food, which is prepared in accordance with these regulations. The Torah outlines the principles of kashrut, including:

Separation of Meat and Dairy

One of the fundamental rules of kashrut is the separation of meat and dairy products. Observant Jews maintain separate utensils, dishes, and cooking surfaces for meat and dairy items to prevent any mingling.

The prohibition against cooking a young goat in its mother's milk is repeated three times in key biblical verses:

Exodus 23:19 (Exodus):

> *"The first of the firstfruits of your ground you shall*
> *bring into the house of the Lord your God. You*
> *shall not boil a young goat in its mother's milk."*

Exodus 34:26 (Exodus):

> *"The best of the firstfruits of your ground you shall*
> *bring to the house of the Lord your God. You*
> *shall not boil a young goat in its mother's milk."*

Deuteronomy 14:21 (Deuteronomy):

> *"You shall not eat anything that has died naturally.*
> *You may give it to the sojourner who is within*
> *your towns, that he may eat it, or you may sell it*
> *to a foreigner. For you are a people holy to the*
> *Lord your God. You shall not boil a young goat*
> *in its mother's milk."*

Over time, Jewish tradition has interpreted these verses to mean a general prohibition against mixing meat and dairy products.

Kosher Slaughter

The ritual slaughter of animals, known as shechita, is performed by a trained, religiously observant individual. The process ensures that the animal is slaughtered humanely and in accordance with Jewish law.

Forbidden Animals

Certain animals, such as pigs and shellfish, are considered unclean and are not permitted. Jews are also prohibited from consuming the blood of animals.

Inspection of Fruits and Vegetables

Fruits and vegetables are subject to inspection to ensure that they are free from insects and other contaminants.

Blessings and Intention

Before consuming food, Jews recite blessings over it to sanctify the act of eating and acknowledge God's role as the ultimate provider.

Kashrut is not only about dietary restrictions but also about fostering mindfulness, discipline, and a deeper connection to God through the act of eating. Kosher food is a manifestation of these principles and serves as a reminder of the importance of maintaining a holy and ethical lifestyle.

LIFECYCLE EVENTS: MARKING SIGNIFICANT MOMENTS

Judaism has many customs and rituals that mark the milestones and significant moments in a person's life. These events are woven into the fabric of Jewish tradition and underscore the importance of continuity, community, and spirituality.

Circumcision (Brit Milah)

A brit milah, or ritual circumcision, is performed on Jewish boys on the eighth day of their lives, by a trained religious practitioner called a mohel, symbolizing the covenant between God and the Jewish people as established with Abraham. The ceremony is often followed by a festive meal, highlighting the communal and family support of the child's entry into the Jewish community.

Bar Mitzvah and Bat Mitzvah

These coming-of-age rituals mark the transition to adulthood for Jewish boys (bar mitzvah) at age 13 and girls (bat mitzvah) at age 12. During these ceremonies, they are called to the Torah for an aliyah, recite blessings, and may lead or participate in synagogue services. The occasion is often celebrated with a festive meal or reception.

Weddings (Kiddushin)

A Jewish wedding is a sacred and joyous occasion, with traditional customs including the signing of the ketubah (marriage contract), the chuppah (wedding canopy), the exchange of rings, and the recitation of blessings. The ceremony is followed by a celebratory feast.

Funerals and Mourning (Avelut)

Jewish funerals follow a specific set of customs and traditions. The deceased is buried promptly after death, and eulogies and prayers are recited. The mourners observe a period of mourning, with practices such as shiva (seven days of mourning), shloshim (thirty days of mourning), and the recitation of the Kaddish prayer to honor the deceased.

These lifecycle events serve not only as personal milestones but also as opportunities to celebrate, reflect, and connect with the larger Jewish community. They reinforce the sense of continuity and responsibility that characterizes Jewish identity.

DID YOU KNOW?

The climactic moment in any Jewish wedding is the part when the groom stamps his foot to smash a glass, right before the ceremonial first kiss as husband and wife. Everyone shouts 'Mazal Tov' ("Congratulations!") and gets ready to party!

It's traditional at most Jewish weddings for the Rabbi or Chazan (Cantor) to sing a Hebrew song called Im Eshkakech Yerushalayim, or in English... 'If I forget you, Jerusalem'. This commemorates the falling of Jerusalem and destruction of the two Jewish temples that once stood there. It also said that breaking of the glass symbolizes the fragility of relation-ships and reminds believers to treat relationships with special care.

THE MEZUZAH: A SYMBOL OF JEWISH FAITH, IDENTITY, AND COMMITMENT

The practice of affixing a mezuzah to the doorpost of Jewish homes and some Jewish-owned businesses is a significant and ancient tradition in Judaism. The mezuzah, a small parchment scroll encased in a decorative container, typically made of wood, metal, or other materials, contains verses from the Torah. This practice holds deep religious and cultural significance for Jewish people and serves several purposes:

Biblical Commandment

The practice of placing a mezuzah on the doorpost is derived from the Torah itself. The biblical commandment is found in the Book of Deuteronomy (Deuteronomy 6:4-9 and Deuteronomy 11:13-21), which includes the famous Shema prayer: "Hear, O Israel, the Lord our God, the Lord is one." The passage instructs Jews to love God with all their heart and soul, to teach God's commandments to their children, and to "write them on the doorposts of your houses and on your gates." The mezuzah serves as a tangible fulfillment of this commandment.

Expression of Faith

Affixing a mezuzah to the doorpost is a visible and symbolic expression of Jewish faith and commitment to God's commandments. It serves as a daily reminder of the central Jewish belief in the oneness of God and the importance of living in accordance with God's teachings.

Protection and Blessing

The mezuzah is often believed to provide protection and blessings to the occupants of the home. It is seen as a spiritual safeguard against negative influences and a source of divine protection for the inhabitants.

Entrance and Exit Ritual

Jews traditionally touch the mezuzah and kiss their fingers after touching it when entering or leaving a room with a mezuzah. This ritual is a way to acknowledge God's presence and seek a connection with the divine as they move in and out of the space.

Jewish Identity and Heritage

Mezuzahs serve as markers of Jewish identity and heritage. They are a distinctive feature of Jewish homes, indicating to visitors and passersby that the residents are Jewish and that Jewish traditions are upheld within the household.

Community and Tradition

The practice of affixing a mezuzah has been passed down through generations, creating a sense of continuity and connection to the Jewish community and tradition.

While the mezuzah is traditionally placed on the doorpost of the main entrance to a Jewish home, it is not affixed to interior doors or doors leading to bathrooms. The mezuzah is carefully prepared and inscribed with the verses from the Torah, and its placement is a ritual act with specific guidelines.

SYNAGOGUE WORSHIP AND PRAYER SERVICES: COMMUNAL AND INDIVIDUAL DEVOTION

Synagogue worship and prayer services are integral to Jewish life and spirituality, providing a framework for both individual and communal devotion. They are not only places of prayer but also centers of learning, community, and social connection.

Synagogues vary in architectural styles and practices, but they typically contain an ark (a cabinet where the Torah scrolls are stored), a bimah (a raised platform from which the Torah is read), and seating for congregants.

Synagogue worship and prayer services include:

Daily Prayer
Jews engage in daily prayer, with prescribed prayer services such as Shaharit (morning prayers), Minchah (afternoon prayers), and Ma'ariv (evening prayers).

Shabbat and Holiday Services
Special prayer services are held on Shabbat and Jewish holidays, with the Torah reading and communal participation.

High Holiday Services
Rosh Hashanah (Jewish New Year) and Yom Kippur (Day of Atonement) feature extended and solemn prayer services, including the sounding of the shofar (ram's horn) on Rosh Hashanah.

Torah Reading
During services, a designated individual, known as a ba'al kriah, reads from the Torah, the sacred scroll containing the first five books of the Hebrew Bible. The Torah is read in a cycle, with different sections read each week.

The Ark and Bimah
The Ark is a sacred cabinet in the synagogue that houses the Torah scrolls, and the Bimah is an elevated platform from which the Torah is read and where the rabbi delivers sermons.

Prayer Books (Siddur)

Siddurim are prayer books that contain the liturgy and text for Jewish prayers, including the Amidah (the central prayer of Jewish worship) and other blessings.

Synagogue worship not only provides a structured approach to prayer but also fosters a sense of community, unity, and spiritual connection among congregants. It is a place where Jews come together to seek God's presence and to find support and inspiration in their faith.

Jewish practices and customs serve as a tapestry of tradition that connects Jewish individuals to their faith, community, and history. Whether through Shabbat observance, dietary laws (kashrut), lifecycle events, or synagogue worship and prayer services, these customs imbue Jewish life with holiness, meaning, and a sense of belonging to a vibrant and enduring tradition.

DID YOU KNOW?

Jews often rock back and forth during prayer, in a practice called "shuckling" from the Yiddish word for "shaking." It's a meditative movement, a swaying forward and back (or side to side) that Jews have been doing while praying or studying since at least the eighth century and possibly since the time of the Talmud. It is said to increase concentration and emotional intensity.

In some Orthodox and Hasidic communities, shuckling is a common and highly visible practice, while in more liberal

Jewish denominations, it may be less prevalent or less pronounced.

Source: https://www.letterstojosep.com/2015/08/18/15-weird-things-jews-do/

While Hebrew is the primary liturgical language of Judaism, Yiddish and Ladino are historical languages associated with Jewish communities. Yiddish developed in Eastern Europe and Ladino in Sephardic Jewish communities.

Jews have several kinds of religious clothing, such as the the tallit, a prayer shawl worn during prayer services. Tallits also have distinctive designs called tzitzit, knotted fringes or tassels at each corner of the shawl.

6

PHILOSOPHY AND THEOLOGY: EXPLORING THE DEPTHS OF FAITH

J ewish philosophy and theology encompass a vast array of ideas, beliefs, and interpretations that have evolved over millennia. These philosophical and theological aspects of Judaism provide insight into its core principles, the various denominations within the Jewish community, the concept of chosenness and covenant, Jewish ethics and moral principles, and the mystical tradition of Kabbalah. Let's delve into these rich and complex facets of Jewish thought and faith.

DIFFERENT JEWISH DENOMINATIONS: VARIETIES OF BELIEF AND PRACTICE

Judaism is not a monolithic tradition but rather a diverse tapestry of beliefs, practices, and interpretations. Various denominations within Judaism reflect a range of perspectives on religious observance, interpretation of Jewish law (Halakha), and the role of tradition in modern life. Some of the major Jewish denominations include:

Orthodox Judaism

Orthodox Judaism is characterized by its strict adherence to traditional Jewish religious law (Halakha) and its conservative approach to religious interpretation. It places a strong emphasis on preserving Jewish customs, rituals, and beliefs as they have been practiced for centuries.

Orthodox Jews believe that the Torah was directly revealed by God to Moses on Mount Sinai and therefore has a steadfast commitment to the unchanging nature of the Torah and Halakha..

Orthodox synagogues often follow traditional prayer customs and are gender-segregated, with separate sections for men and women.

Orthodox Judaism is further divided into Modern Orthodox and Ultra-Orthodox (Haredi) streams, each with its own approach to engaging with the modern world.

Conservative Judaism

Conservative Judaism seeks to strike a balance between tradition and modernity. It emerged in the mid-19th century as a response to the challenges posed by the modern world. It adheres to Jewish law but allows for some flexibility in interpreting and applying it, considering contemporary ethical concerns.

It also strives to be inclusive, welcoming both men and women as equals in religious life. This includes the ordination of female rabbis and the recognition of LGBTQ+ individuals.

Reform Judaism

Reform Judaism emphasizes individual autonomy in religious practice and belief. Similarly to Conservative Judaism, it emerged in the 19th century with the goal of modernizing and adapting Jewish practice to contemporary life.

It embraces a more liberal and modern approach to religious practice and interpretation. It places an emphasis on evolving and adapting Judaism to be relevant to the contemporary world.

While Reform Jews revere the Torah, they approach its interpretation in a more flexible manner, often using a historical-critical approach and considering the evolving context of Jewish life.

It is known for its openness to diversity and inclusivity. It is welcoming of Jews from diverse backgrounds, as well as interfaith families and LGBTQ+ individuals.

Reconstructionist Judaism

Reconstructionism emerged in the early 20th century in the United States. Founded by Rabbi Mordecai Kaplan, Reconstructionism represents a significant departure from traditional Jewish beliefs and practices.

It emphasizes Judaism as an evolving and evolving civilization, encompassing not only religious beliefs but also cultural, historical, and ethical aspects. It views Judaism as an ethnic and cultural identity, not solely a religious one.

Reconstructionist Judaism does not necessarily adhere to traditional beliefs in a personal, anthropomorphic God. Instead, God is often seen as a symbol, representing a unifying force in the universe or a concept that inspires moral and ethical behavior.

It prioritizes the role of the Jewish community as the central locus of Jewish life. Congregations and communities have a significant say in shaping their religious practices and rituals.

Reconstructionist Jews believe that Jewish tradition is a dynamic entity that evolves over time. They are open to adapting customs, rituals, and practices to reflect contemporary values and changing social norms.

Hassidic Judaism

Orthodox Judaism known for its fervent spirituality, mysticism, and distinct religious practices. It emerged in the 18th century in Eastern Europe, and its teachings and customs continue to influence the lives of Hasidic Jews today.

It emphasizes joy in worship, religious fervor, and the importance of the tzaddik, a righteous leader.

Hasidic Jews are known for their distinctive dress, which varies by community. Men typically wear long black coats, black hats, and long sidelocks (payot), while married women often cover their hair with wigs or scarves.

They place a strong emphasis on Torah study, and many communities have their own yeshivas (Jewish religious schools) where young men study Jewish texts intensively.

Hasidic prayer services are characterized by melodious singing, swaying, and heartfelt devotion. Congregational prayer is essential, and Hasidic Jews aim to infuse joy and fervor into their worship.

The tzaddik (righteous leader) is a revered figure in Hasidic Judaism. The tzaddik is believed to possess extraordinary spiritual insight and is seen as a conduit to God.

These denominations represent the diversity of Jewish thought and practice, with varying degrees of adherence to tradition and interpretation of religious texts.

THE CONCEPT OF CHOSENNESS AND COVENANT: A UNIQUE RELATIONSHIP WITH GOD

Central to Jewish theology is the concept of chosenness and covenant. According to Jewish belief, God chose the Jewish people to enter into a unique covenant, a sacred and binding agreement that entails both privileges and responsibilities.

Key elements of the concept of chosenness and covenant include:

Abrahamic Covenant
The covenant was initiated with Abraham, who was chosen to be the father of the Jewish people. God promised to make his descendants a great nation.

Sinai Covenant
The covenant was further solidified at Mount Sinai when the Israelites received the Torah, a set of divine instructions. The Jewish people committed to following God's laws, and God promised to protect and bless them.

Responsibility and Ethical Obligation
Chosenness does not imply superiority but rather a unique role in serving as a "light to the nations." The Jewish people are called to live by ethical principles and set an example for the world.

The concept of chosenness and covenant underscores the Jewish commitment to following God's laws and living ethically. It is not about exclusivity but about living with purpose and responsibility.

JEWISH ETHICS AND MORAL PRINCIPLES: A BLUEPRINT FOR RIGHTEOUS LIVING

Jewish ethics and moral principles form the ethical framework that guides Jewish behavior and interactions with others. Rooted in the Torah and rabbinic teachings, Jewish ethics emphasize values such as justice, compassion, humility, and kindness.

Let's look at some of these ethical principles.

Tikkun Olam

Tikkun olam means "repairing the world." It calls on Jews to engage in acts of social justice and to work towards making the world a better place. This concept is central to Reform and liberal Jewish traditions.

Tzedakah

Tzedakah, often translated as "charity," is the obligation to give to those in need. It is seen as an act of righteousness and social justice.

Gemilut Chasadim

Gemilut chasadim means "acts of loving-kindness." It encompasses actions such as visiting the sick, comforting mourners, and providing for the needs of others.

Lashon Hara

Lashon hara is the prohibition against speaking ill of others or engaging in harmful gossip.

Honesty and Integrity
Honesty and integrity are highly valued, with a strong emphasis on fair business practices and truthfulness in speech.

Jewish ethics provide a moral compass for daily life, emphasizing the importance of ethical behavior, social responsibility, and the pursuit of justice.

JEWISH MYSTICISM (KABBALAH): THE HIDDEN DIMENSIONS OF FAITH

Kabbalah is the mystical and esoteric tradition within Judaism, offering insights into the hidden, spiritual aspects of God and the universe. Kabbalistic teachings explore themes such as the sefirot (divine emanations), the Ein Sof (infinite God), and the quest for spiritual enlightenment.

Sefirot
The sefirot are ten attributes or emanations of God that represent different aspects of divine energy and wisdom.

Ein Sof
Ein Sof is the concept of the infinite and unknowable God, transcending all human comprehension.

Merkavah Mysticism

Merkavah mysticism focuses on mystical encounters with God's chariot (merkavah) and visionary experiences.

Practical Kabbalah

Practical Kabbalah delves into the application of mystical teachings in daily life, including meditative and magical practices.

Kabbalah offers a deeper, more spiritual dimension to Jewish thought, providing insights into the nature of God and the human soul. It has been a source of inspiration for Jewish mystics and scholars throughout history.

In summary, Jewish philosophy and theology encompass a wide spectrum of beliefs, denominations, concepts, and traditions that have shaped Jewish thought and practice over millennia. These aspects of Judaism reflect the diversity and depth of Jewish faith, guiding adherents in their relationship with God, ethical living, and the pursuit of spiritual enlightenment.

7

THE SPREAD OF JUDAISM AND THE JEWISH DIASPORA: A GLOBAL JOURNEY

The spread of Judaism, its global diaspora, and the dispersion of Jewish communities have been central to its story. This journey, spanning over two millennia, has brought Jewish culture, faith, and identity to various regions across the world. Let's take a look into the history of the Jewish diaspora, the influence of Judaism in different regions, and the challenges and opportunities of maintaining Jewish identity in diverse contexts.

THE JEWISH DIASPORA: A HISTORICAL OVERVIEW

The Jewish diaspora, or the dispersion of Jewish communities outside of the historical land of Israel, has its roots in ancient times. The earliest instances of Jewish diaspora occurred due to exile, conquest, and forced migrations, notably the Babylonian exile in the 6th century BCE. However, the most significant and defining moment in the history of the Jewish diaspora was the Roman destruction of the Second Temple in 70 CE, which led to widespread Jewish dispersal throughout the Roman Empire.

The Jewish diaspora can be divided into several key phases and regions:

Roman Diaspora
After the fall of Jerusalem and the destruction of the Second Temple, Jews were dispersed across the Roman Empire, from North Africa to Europe, the Middle East, and beyond. This dispersion laid the foundation for the establishment of Jewish communities in these regions.

Medieval Dispersal
During the Middle Ages, Jewish communities flourished in Europe, particularly in Spain, France, and Germany. They faced periods of persecution and expulsion, such as the Spanish Inquisition, leading to further dispersion to the Ottoman Empire, North Africa, and Eastern Europe.

Eastern Diaspora
In parallel with the Roman diaspora, Jewish communities also settled in the Middle East and Asia. The Babylonian exile led to the establishment of a thriving Jewish center in Babylonia (modern-day Iraq). Jewish communities also

formed in India, Yemen, and Iran, each with its unique traditions.

Modern Dispersal
The rise of modernity and the spread of Enlightenment ideas in the 18th century prompted Jewish migrations to new destinations, including North America and Western Europe. Jewish communities also continued to grow in regions like Argentina, South Africa, and Australia.

Zionist Movement and Israel
The late 19th and early 20th centuries saw the rise of the Zionist movement, which sought to establish a Jewish homeland in Israel. In 1948, the State of Israel was established, leading to the ingathering of Jewish communities from around the world.

INFLUENCE OF JUDAISM IN VARIOUS REGIONS

The Jewish diaspora has left an indelible mark on the regions where Jewish communities have settled, contributing to the cultural, social, and intellectual development of their host societies. Here, we explore the influence of Judaism in Europe, the Middle East, and North America.

Europe

Jewish communities have a long and complex history in Europe. In medieval Europe, Jews played significant roles in trade, finance, and scholarship. They also contributed to the

Renaissance and Enlightenment movements. Yiddish, a fusion of Hebrew and German, became a distinct language in Eastern Europe, reflecting the Jewish cultural influence in the region.

However, Europe also witnessed anti-Semitic persecutions, expulsions, and the Holocaust during World War II, leading to the decimation of Jewish communities in Eastern Europe with over 6 million killed by the Nazis. After the war, many survivors and refugees emigrated to North America, shaping the vibrant Jewish culture there.

The Middle East

Jews have a historical presence in the Middle East dating back to ancient times. The Babylonian exile in the 6th century BCE led to the establishment of the Babylonian Talmud, one of the most significant works of Jewish scholarship. Jewish communities in the Middle East, particularly in Iraq, Iran, and Yemen, have rich and distinct traditions, including unique culinary, musical, and linguistic elements.

The establishment of the State of Israel in 1948 had a profound impact on the Middle East, reshaping geopolitical dynamics and affecting the relationships between Jewish and non-Jewish communities in the region.

North America

Jews arrived in North America as early as the colonial period. Over time, Jewish communities have thrived in the United States and Canada, making significant contributions to various fields, including politics, business, the arts, and academia.

North America has witnessed the development of diverse Jewish denominations, from Orthodox to Reform to Conservative, reflecting the pluralistic nature of Jewish religious practice. Jewish culture, including the celebration of Jewish holidays, has been integrated into the broader tapestry of American and Canadian life.

CHALLENGES AND OPPORTUNITIES OF MAINTAINING JEWISH IDENTITY IN DIFFERENT CONTEXTS

The Jewish diaspora has posed various challenges and opportunities for maintaining Jewish identity in diverse contexts. Some of the key factors include:

Assimilation and Acculturation
Jews living in diaspora regions often face the challenge of assimilation into the dominant culture. The opportunities for education, economic advancement, and social integration may lead to acculturation. Maintaining Jewish identity can be a delicate balance between adapting to the host culture and preserving Jewish traditions.

Preservation of Tradition
Jewish communities have displayed remarkable resilience in preserving their religious and cultural traditions in diaspora

settings. Synagogues, Jewish schools, and community organizations play a vital role in transmitting Jewish values, language, and rituals to future generations.

Intermarriage

Interfaith marriages, while providing opportunities for cultural exchange, can also raise questions about the continuity of Jewish identity. Jewish communities have debated strategies to address this issue, including outreach and education programs.

Anti-Semitism

In various periods and places, Jews have faced discrimination, persecution, and anti-Semitic violence. The enduring challenge of anti-Semitism necessitates vigilance in preserving Jewish identity while safeguarding the safety and security of Jewish communities. We look at this in more detail in Chapter 9.

Innovation and Adaptation

Jewish communities in the diaspora have demonstrated remarkable adaptability and innovation. They have embraced new technologies, engaged with broader societal issues, and fostered a dynamic culture of Jewish learning and expression.

Israel and the Homeland Connection

For many Jewish communities, the State of Israel serves as a unifying element that connects diaspora Jews to their homeland. The relationship between diaspora Jews and Israel is both a source of identity and a subject of complex and ongoing discussions.

The Jewish diaspora represents a remarkable journey of survival, adaptation, and contribution to various regions of the world. Jewish communities have faced challenges to their identity but have also seized opportunities for cultural exchange, education, and innovation. The Jewish diaspora continues to be a dynamic and evolving phenomenon, reflecting the enduring nature of Jewish culture, faith, and tradition

8

CULTURE AND TRADITIONS: A TAPESTRY OF HERITAGE

J ewish culture and traditions are a rich and diverse tapestry woven over thousands of years. This heritage encompasses a wide range of expressions, from art, music, and literature to festivals, holidays, and the importance of preserving and passing down Jewish traditions. Let's take a look at Jewish culture, highlighting the significance of each component in the context of Jewish identity and continuity.

JEWISH ART, MUSIC, AND LITERATURE: EXPRESSIONS OF IDENTITY AND FAITH

Jewish culture is full of artistic, musical, and literary expressions that reflect the identity, faith, and history of the Jewish people. These forms of creativity have evolved over centuries, providing a lens through which to understand the multifaceted nature of Jewish culture.

Jewish Art

Jewish art has a long history that includes various styles and forms. Historically, Jewish art was characterized by intricate religious objects, illuminated manuscripts, and synagogue decorations. Over time, Jewish artists have drawn inspiration from their own traditions and the cultures in which they lived.

Illuminated Manuscripts
Jewish scribes have created beautifully illustrated manuscripts of religious texts, such as the Torah and the Haggadah (used during Passover Seder).

Synagogue Decorations
Synagogues have often been adorned with intricate mosaics, frescoes, and stained glass that convey religious and historical themes.

Contemporary Art
Jewish artists today engage with a wide range of artistic styles and themes. Their work often explores the complexities of identity, history, and Jewish traditions.

JEWISH MUSIC

Jewish music encompasses a vast array of genres and styles, reflecting the diversity of Jewish communities around the world. It plays a central role in religious, communal, and cultural life.

Cantorial Music
Cantors lead synagogue services with soulful and melodic renditions of liturgical texts. Nusach, or traditional melodies, vary among Jewish denominations.

Klezmer Music
Klezmer is a lively, instrumental music traditionally played at Jewish celebrations, particularly weddings. It has a distinct, Eastern European flavor.

Liturgical and Folk Songs
Jewish liturgy includes a range of hymns and melodies. Additionally, there are numerous Jewish folk songs that reflect everyday life and communal experiences.

Contemporary Jewish Music
Contemporary Jewish musicians continue to explore and innovate in a variety of styles, from folk and rock to hip-hop and reggae.

Jewish literature is marked by religious and cultural themes. It encompasses a wide range of genres, from sacred texts to novels, poetry, and philosophical treatises.

The Torah and Talmud

The Torah, the central sacred text of Judaism, is complemented by the Talmud, an extensive commentary and interpretation of Jewish law and tradition.

Yiddish Literature

Yiddish, a language developed by Ashkenazi Jews, is associated with a rich literary tradition, including works by authors like Sholem Aleichem and Isaac Bashevis Singer.

Holocaust Literature

The Holocaust has had a profound impact on Jewish literature. Works such as Elie Wiesel's "Night" and Primo Levi's "Survival in Auschwitz" bear witness to the Holocaust's horrors.

Modern Jewish Literature

Contemporary Jewish authors continue to explore themes of identity, assimilation, and the complexities of Jewish life in their works.

Jewish art, music, and literature serve as vehicles for preserving and transmitting Jewish identity, history, and culture. They provide a means for reflection, celebration, and the exploration of profound themes that resonate across generations.

JEWISH FESTIVALS AND HOLIDAYS: CELEBRATING HISTORY AND FAITH

Jewish festivals and holidays are a central aspect of Jewish culture, as both religious observances and opportunities for communal celebration. These occasions are deeply rooted in history, faith, and tradition, and they play a vital role in preserving Jewish culture and identity.

Passover (Pesach)

Passover is a spring festival that commemorates the Israelites' liberation from slavery in Egypt. It is observed with a festive Seder meal that includes the retelling of the Exodus story and the consumption of symbolic foods, including matzah (unleavened bread) and bitter herbs. Passover serves as a powerful reminder of Jewish resilience and the pursuit of freedom.

Hanukkah

Hanukkah, often referred to as the Festival of Lights celebrates the Maccabee's victory over the Syrian-Greek rulers of Jerusalem and the Temple's rededication in 164 BCE. The holiday lasts eight days, and it is celebrated by lighting the menorah, eating foods fried in oil, and playing the dreidel game. Jewish families light eight candles over eight days. On day one they light one candle, on day two they light two candles, etc. Hanukkah represents the triumph of light over darkness and the resilience of the Jewish spirit.

Although Hanukkah is an important Jewish holiday, it is not part of the Hebrew Scriptures because it celebrates an event that occurred after the Scriptures were written.

Rosh Hashanah and Yom Kippur

Rosh Hashanah, the Jewish New Year, is a time for reflection and introspection. It is marked by the sounding of the shofar (ram's horn) and the beginning of the Ten Days of Repentance, which culminate in Yom Kippur, the Day of Atonement. Yom Kippur is a day of fasting and prayer, with the central focus on repentance, forgiveness, and spiritual renewal.

Sukkot

Sukkot is a harvest festival that involves the construction of temporary outdoor shelters (sukkot) and the waving of the Four Species: the lulav (palm branch), etrog (citron), myrtle, and willow. It celebrates the Jews' wandering in the desert after the Exodus.

Shavuot

Shavuot marks the giving of the Torah at Mount Sinai and the harvest of the first fruits. It is observed through Torah study, the reading of the Book of Ruth, and the eating of dairy foods.

Purim

Purim is a joyous festival that commemorates the salvation of the Jewish people from a plot to destroy them in ancient Persia, as recounted in the Book of Esther. It is celebrated with reading the Megillah (Book of Esther), wearing costumes, and giving gifts to the needy.

Sabbath (Shabbat)

While not a festival, Shabbat is a weekly observance that plays a central role in Jewish life. It is a day of rest, spiritual rejuvenation, and communal gatherings, marked by the lighting of candles and festive meals.

Jewish festivals and holidays are not only religious observances but also cultural celebrations that bring families and communities together. They offer opportunities for storytelling, song, dance, and the passing down of traditions from one generation to the next.

THE IMPORTANCE OF PRESERVING AND PASSING DOWN JEWISH TRADITIONS

The preservation and transmission of Jewish traditions are central to the continuity and vitality of Jewish culture and identity. Several key factors highlight their significance:

Historical Continuity
Jewish traditions have endured for millennia, shaping the cultural and religious identity of Jewish communities world-

wide. Preserving these traditions ensures the continuity of Jewish heritage for future generations.

Cultural Memory

Jewish traditions serve as a living memory of Jewish history, including struggles, triumphs, and shared experiences. They help connect Jews to their ancestors and their roots.

Spiritual Significance

Many Jewish traditions are deeply rooted in religious faith and practice. They foster a sense of spirituality, reverence, and connection to God.

Community Cohesion

Jewish traditions foster a sense of belonging and community. Celebrating festivals, observing rituals, and engaging in acts of kindness (mitzvot) strengthen social bonds and promote a shared sense of identity.

Cultural Diversity

The Jewish diaspora has given rise to diverse traditions within the Jewish community, adding to the richness of Jewish culture. The preservation of these diverse traditions contributes to the mosaic of Jewish identity.

Ethical Values

Jewish traditions often convey ethical values and principles that guide individuals in their daily lives. The transmission of these values promotes moral and ethical conduct.

Education and Learning

The passing down of Jewish traditions involves education and the study of sacred texts. Jewish learning is a lifelong pursuit that deepens one's understanding of tradition and faith.

Jewish culture and traditions encompass a multifaceted tapestry of artistic expression, music, literature, festivals, and holidays. These aspects of Jewish life are deeply intertwined with faith, history, and identity.

DID YOU KNOW?

Jews have made significant contributions to various fields, including science, philosophy, literature, art, and music.

In science, Albert Einstein, developed the theory of relativity, while Jonas Salk, a medical researcher, developed the polio vaccine.

Sigmund Freud, the founder of psychoanalysis, revolutionized the field of psychology. Jewish authors and philosophers, such as Franz Kafka and Martin Buber, have produced influential works exploring human existence and societal issues.

In the arts, Jewish musicians, composers, and actors, including Bob Dylan, Leonard Bernstein, and Barbra Streisand, have achieved great acclaim.

Source:

https://www.havefunwithhistory.com/facts-about-judaism/

9

CONTEMPORARY ISSUES: JUDAISM IN THE MODERN WORLD

J udaism, like all major religions, faces a range of contemporary issues as it navigates the challenges and opportunities of the modern world. These challenges include debates within the Jewish community, assimilation, interfaith relations, the complex dynamics surrounding Israel, and the role of Judaism in social justice and humanitarian causes.

ANTI-SEMITISM

Anti-Semitism is the prejudice, discrimination, and hostility directed against Jewish individuals or Jewish communities. This form of hatred and bias has a long and dark history, persisting in various forms throughout the modern world. It is essential to understand what anti-Semitism is, why it remains prevalent, and why Jews have been persecuted throughout history to combat this injustice and work towards a more inclusive and tolerant society.

Anti-Semitism encompasses a range of discriminatory beliefs and actions, including stereotypes, slurs, violence, and even acts of terrorism. It is rooted in irrational prejudice and conspiracy theories that falsely portray Jews as malevolent or threatening. Anti-Semitic sentiments have manifested in political, social, and religious spheres, making them a pervasive and harmful force.

HISTORICAL PERSECUTION OF JEWS

Throughout history, Jewish people have been persecuted, causing death and waves of refugees and the formation of diaspora communities. As early as 606 BCE, Jews living in the Neo-Babylonian Empire were persecuted and expelled. Anti-semitism was widespread in the Roman Empire, in Christianity and in many regions of the world including the Middle East.

Some of the most well-known massacres of Jews include:

Granada Massacre of 1066

On December 30, 1066, a Muslim mob stormed the royal palace in Granada and killed more than 1,000 Jewish families. The group also kidnapped and crucified Joseph ibn Naghrela, the Jewish vizier to the Berber king.

The First Crusade

In the first of the Crusades - a series of medieval holy wars involving Christians and Muslims - thousands of Jews were killed, and many were forced to convert to Christianity.

The Massacre at Clifford's Tower

One of the worst anti-Semitic massacres of the Middle Ages took place in York in England, in 1190. The city's entire Jewish community was trapped by an angry mob inside the tower of York Castle. Many members of the community chose to commit suicide rather than be murdered or forcibly baptized by the attackers.

The growing hostility towards the Jewish population in England, was in part due to public disagreements in theology between Jewish scholars and Christian churchmen. In the mid-12th century several vicious stories were spread accusing Jews of murdering Christian children. Such slanders, now known as the 'Blood Libel', strengthened anti-Semitic sentiment in England.

The Spanish Expulsion

In 1492, Spain's rulers issued a royal edict that declared all Jews who refused to convert to Christianity would be expelled from the country. Experts estimate about 200,000 people were ousted and tens of thousands died while trying to reach safety.

The Holocaust

The Holocaust, in which six million Jews were systematically murdered by the Nazis during World War II, represents one of the most horrific instances of anti-Semitic persecution in history.

DID YOU KNOW?

In 1290, the entire Jewish population of England (about 3,000 people) was expelled from the country on the orders of Edward I.

Source:
https://www.history.ox.ac.uk/why-were-the-jews-expelled-from-england-in-1290-0

Reasons for this persecution include:

Religious Differences
In the Middle Ages, many Christians, including members of the clergy, held the Jewish people collectively responsible for the killing of Jesus. This not only extended to those Jews present at the time of Jesus' death, but for all time, having commited the sin of deicide, or 'god-killing'. This has led to 1,900 years of hatred, violence and murder of Jews.

Economic Envy
Jews have faced economic persecution, with resentment over

their success in trade and finance leading to discriminatory laws, expulsions, and the seizure of Jewish property.

Blood Libel

The false accusation that Jews used the blood of Christian children for ritual purposes, known as blood libel, led to massacres and pogroms in Europe.

Zionism and Israel

Opposition to the State of Israel's existence and its policies has sometimes manifested as anti-Semitism, with Jews being targeted for their perceived connection to Israel.

Conspiracy Theories

Jews have been targeted by conspiracy theories that allege secret Jewish control of the world, which can lead to discrimination and violence.

Combating anti-Semitism requires raising awareness, promoting education, and fostering tolerance. Addressing the root causes and challenging stereotypes and discrimination are vital steps in the ongoing effort to eradicate anti-Semitism and create a more inclusive and equitable world.

Stereotypes and Myths

Anti-Semitism often relies on harmful stereotypes, such as the portrayal of Jews as manipulative, greedy, or responsible for societal problems. Myths about Jewish control of the media or world financial systems continue to circulate.

Hate Speech

Online platforms and social media have facilitated the spread of anti-Semitic hate speech, including Holocaust denial, Holocaust revisionism, and the dissemination of conspiracy theories.

Violence

Jews have been targeted in violent attacks, from physical assaults to vandalism of synagogues and Jewish cemeteries.

Boycotts and Discrimination

Calls for boycotts of Jewish businesses and academic institutions, as well as academic and professional discrimination against Jews, have been used as forms of economic and social punishment.

CHALLENGES AND DEBATES WITHIN THE JEWISH COMMUNITY

The Jewish community is not monolithic; it comprises a diverse range of religious beliefs, denominations, and cultural backgrounds. These diversities often lead to debates on various issues. Some of the key challenges and debates within the Jewish community include:

Assimilation

Assimilation is a persistent concern among Jewish communities around the world. The fear of losing Jewish identity due to intermarriage, secularization, or external cultural influences remains a topic of discussion and debate. Some groups advocate for outreach efforts to engage assimilated Jews, while others emphasize maintaining strict religious boundaries.

Interfaith Relations

Judaism has a long history of interaction with other religious traditions. Interfaith dialogue and cooperation, particularly with Christianity and Islam, are crucial aspects of contemporary Jewish life. However, these engagements are not without challenges, as differences in theology and historical tensions can create complex dynamics. The quest for mutual understanding and respect is an ongoing effort.

Israel: Political and Religious Dimensions

Israel holds a central place in contemporary Jewish identity and politics. Debates surrounding Israeli policies, the Israeli-Palestinian conflict, and the role of religion in the state often spark passionate discussions. Different Jewish denominations and organizations take varying positions on these issues, reflecting the diversity of views within the Jewish community.

Gender and Religious Leadership
Gender equality within Jewish religious leadership has been an ongoing debate. Orthodox Judaism traditionally adheres to a gendered division of roles, while Reform and Conservative Judaism have made strides in promoting women's participation in religious leadership. This issue reflects broader societal discussions on gender and religion.

Conversion and Inclusivity
The process of conversion to Judaism and questions of inclusivity have become significant points of discussion. Many Jewish communities are wrestling with how to be more inclusive to converts, those of mixed heritage, and those who have been historically marginalized.

ASSIMILATION AND THE PRESERVATION OF JEWISH IDENTITY

The issue of assimilation is one of the most significant challenges facing the Jewish community. Assimilation occurs when individuals and families adopt the customs, traditions, and values of the broader culture in which they live. In the

Jewish context, assimilation often includes intermarriage with non-Jews, secularization, and a decline in religious observance. The concerns regarding assimilation include:

Cultural and Religious Preservation
Assimilation raises concerns about the preservation of Jewish cultural and religious traditions. There is a fear that as Jews assimilate into broader society, they may lose their connection to their heritage and identity.

Continuity of Tradition
Assimilation can affect the continuity of Jewish traditions, as many Jews may choose to forego Jewish rituals and practices. The passing down of traditions from one generation to the next may weaken.

Intermarriage
The rate of intermarriage, particularly in the United States, has increased. While it can be a source of enrichment through cultural exchange, it also raises questions about the future of Jewish identity within mixed-faith families.

Responses
Responses to assimilation vary. Some segments of the Jewish community advocate for outreach and education to engage assimilated Jews, while others emphasize maintaining religious boundaries to preserve Jewish identity.

INTERFAITH RELATIONS AND DIALOGUE

Interfaith relations are a critical aspect of Jewish engagement with the modern world. Judaism has a history of interaction with other religious traditions, and contemporary interfaith efforts aim to promote mutual understanding and cooperation. Key points regarding interfaith relations include:

Dialogue and Cooperation
Jewish organizations engage in interfaith dialogue and cooperation with other religious communities, particularly Christianity and Islam. These efforts promote peace, understanding, and shared values.

Challenges
Interfaith relations are not without challenges, as differences in theology and historical tensions can create complex dynamics. Addressing these issues requires openness, patience, and a commitment to mutual respect.

Social Justice and Ethics
Interfaith efforts often focus on common ethical and social justice concerns. Jews, Christians, and Muslims frequently collaborate on issues such as poverty, environmental stewardship, and human rights.

Interfaith Education
Promoting interfaith education is a key component of fostering positive relations. Schools, religious institutions,

and community organizations often offer interfaith programs to facilitate understanding and cooperation.

THE ISRAELI-PALESTINIAN CONFLICT

The Israeli-Palestinian conflict is a complex and contentious issue with profound political, religious, and ethical dimensions as well as far-reaching implications for Jewish identity. This is particularly important since the Hamas massacre of October 7th, 2023, and the subsequent war in Gaza, on-going at the time of writing.

Diverse Perspectives

The Jewish community is not monolithic in its approach to the Israeli-Palestinian conflict. Different Jewish denominations and organizations take various positions, from strong support for Israel to calls for a more balanced approach to the conflict.

Religious Significance

The land of Israel has deep religious significance for Jews. Debates center on the relationship between religious beliefs, historical narratives, and political realities.

Humanitarian Concerns

Many Jews are deeply committed to humanitarian values and human rights. Concerns about the treatment of Palestinians and the pursuit of a just and lasting peace are central to these discussions.

Dialogue and Peacemaking
Some Jewish organizations actively engage in dialogue and peacemaking efforts, both within the Jewish community and in partnership with Palestinians and others.

The Role of Israel in Jewish Identity
Israel plays a central role in the Jewish identity of many Jews around the world. Its existence, policies, and actions are subjects of ongoing reflection and discussion.

GENDER AND RELIGIOUS LEADERSHIP

The role of women in religious leadership has been a matter of debate in many Jewish denominations.

Orthodox Judaism
Orthodox Judaism traditionally adheres to a gendered division of roles, with men primarily leading religious services and holding positions of religious authority. There has been ongoing discussion about expanding opportunities for women's religious leadership within the bounds of traditional Halakha (Jewish law).

Reform and Conservative Judaism
Reform and Conservative Judaism have made significant strides in promoting gender equality in religious leadership. Women serve as rabbis, cantors, and in various other religious roles in these denominations.

Interdenominational Dialogue
Interdenominational dialogue has facilitated discussions about women's roles in Jewish leadership. There is a growing recognition of the importance of mutual respect and understanding across denominational lines.

Social and Ethical Considerations
Gender equality within religious leadership is not only a religious issue but also a matter of social and ethical significance. It reflects broader societal conversations on gender equity and inclusivity.

CONVERSION AND INCLUSIVITY

Judaism's approach to conversion and inclusivity has evolved and continues to be a topic of debate.

Conversion to Judaism
The process of conversion to Judaism varies among denominations, with differences in requirements and procedures. Debates arise over how to make conversion more accessible and welcoming.

Inclusivity of Marginalized Groups
Jewish communities are increasingly focusing on inclusivity and welcoming marginalized groups, including people of color, LGBTQ+ individuals, and those of mixed heritage.

Debate over Tradition and Change

Conversations around inclusivity often intersect with debates over tradition and change. Jewish communities grapple with how to adapt while maintaining their core values and beliefs.

Embracing Diversity

Embracing diversity and addressing issues of inclusivity are seen as ways to strengthen Jewish communities and ensure their vibrancy in the future.

THE ROLE OF JUDAISM IN SOCIAL JUSTICE AND HUMANITARIAN CAUSES

Judaism places a strong emphasis on ethical values and social justice, motivating Jewish individuals and organizations to engage in various humanitarian causes.

Tikkun Olam

Tikkun olam, the concept of "repairing the world," is central to Jewish ethics. It calls on Jews to engage in acts of social justice, charity, and community service. Tikkun olam is a driving force behind many Jewish humanitarian initiatives.

Charitable Giving

Acts of charity, known as tzedakah, are considered a moral obligation in Judaism. Jewish organizations often provide support to vulnerable populations, addressing issues such as poverty, hunger, and homelessness.

Human Rights Advocacy
Jewish communities have been active in advocating for human rights and social justice, both locally and globally. They support causes such as civil rights, refugee resettlement, and the fight against discrimination.

Environmental Stewardship
The principles of bal tashchit (do not destroy) and shomrei adamah (guardians of the earth) underscore Judaism's commitment to environmental sustainability and protection.

Interfaith and Multifaith Collaboration
Many Jewish organizations engage in interfaith and multifaith initiatives to address social justice concerns. Collaborative efforts with other religious communities amplify the impact of humanitarian work.

Educational Initiatives
Jewish schools and institutions often include social justice and humanitarian education as integral components of their programs. Teaching the values of compassion and justice to future generations is considered vital.

Judaism in the modern world faces a myriad of challenges and opportunities. The debates within the Jewish community, the issue of assimilation, interfaith relations, the complexities surrounding Israel, and the role of Judaism in social justice and humanitarian causes are central to the ongoing conversation within Jewish communities. These discussions reflect the dynamic and evolving nature of Judaism as it engages with the complexities of the contemporary world, seeking to uphold its rich heritage while addressing the pressing issues of our time.

10

CONCLUSION

T hroughout this guide, we have journeyed through the history, beliefs, practices, and cultural aspects of Judaism. We have delved into the rich tapestry of Jewish culture, the importance of preserving traditions, and the dynamic challenges and opportunities that Judaism faces in the modern world.

Judaism, as we have seen, is a religion deeply rooted in tradition, with a history that spans thousands of years. From the foundational texts of the Hebrew Bible, including the Torah, Prophets, and Writings, to the philosophical insights of Maimonides and the mystical depths of Kabbalah, Judaism offers a wealth of wisdom and guidance for its adherents.

Jewish practices and customs, such as the observance of Shabbat, dietary laws, lifecycle events, and synagogue worship, are the threads that bind the Jewish community together. Its wide range of beliefs, practices, and interpretations, reflect the diversity of Jewish communities across the world and is a source of strength, resilience, and richness.

We've looked at the changing nature of Judaism in the contemporary world. The challenges of assimilation, interfaith relations, and the complexities surrounding Israel are ongoing debates within the Jewish community. These discussions reflect the community's adaptability and the commitment to preserving its heritage while engaging with the broader world.

Judaism continues to have a profound impact on the world. Jewish individuals and organizations are actively engaged in various humanitarian initiatives, contributing to the betterment of society at large. The commitment to social justice and humanitarian causes, to make the world a better place is a testament to the enduring ethical values of Judaism.

In a world where understanding and respecting diverse cultures and religions are more critical than ever. We hope this guide has helped in understanding, appreciating, and respecting the multifaceted world of Judaism, its faith, culture, and people, and its contributions to the rich tapestry of human history and civilization.

11

GLOSSARY

Abraham
The patriarch of Judaism, considered the father of the Jewish
people, and a key figure in Jewish history.

Bar/Bat Mitzvah
A Jewish coming-of-age ceremony, typically held at the age
of 13 for boys (Bar Mitzvah) and 12 for girls (Bat Mitzvah),
symbolizing the assumption of religious responsibilities.

Covenant
A sacred agreement or contract between God and the Jewish
people, as described in the Hebrew Bible, particularly in the
Torah.

Diaspora
The dispersion of Jewish communities outside of the histor-

ical land of Israel, which has led to the formation of Jewish communities in various regions around the world.

Exodus
The biblical account of the Israelites' liberation from slavery in Egypt, a central narrative in Jewish history.

Festival
A religious celebration or holiday in Judaism, often marked by special rituals, customs, and observances. Examples include Passover, Hanukkah, and Yom Kippur.

Halakha
The Jewish legal system and code of ethics, encompassing religious laws and traditions that guide Jewish life.

Haggadah
A Jewish text used during the Passover Seder, which tells the story of the Exodus and includes prayers, blessings, and songs.

Kashrut
The Jewish dietary laws and regulations governing what foods are considered kosher (fit or proper) for consumption.

Kippah
A skullcap worn by Jewish men as a sign of reverence and Jewish identity.

Maimonides
Also known as Rambam, a prominent medieval Jewish philosopher, theologian, and physician, known for his "13 Principles of Faith."

Messianic
Related to the concept of the Messiah in Judaism, which refers to a future savior figure who will bring redemption and peace to the world.

Menorah
A seven-branched candelabrum, often associated with Hanukkah and used in Jewish worship and symbolism.

Passover
A major Jewish festival that commemorates the liberation of the Israelites from slavery in Egypt and involves a special Seder meal.

Phylacteries
Also known as tefillin, small boxes containing passages from the Torah that Jewish men wear during weekday morning prayers.

Rabbi
A Jewish religious leader, teacher, and authority on Jewish law and traditions.

Reform Judaism
One of the major denominations of Judaism, characterized
by a more liberal and adaptable approach to Jewish law and
tradition.

Sabbath (Shabbat)
The Jewish day of rest, observed from Friday evening to
Saturday evening, dedicated to rest, worship, and communal
activities.

Seder
A ritual Passover meal, which includes the retelling of the
Exodus story, special foods, and prayers.

Semitic
A term referring to the Semitic language group and the
Semitic peoples, including Jews, Arabs, and others.

Synagogue
A Jewish place of worship and communal gathering for
prayer, study, and religious events.

Talmud
A central text in Rabbinic Judaism, consisting of the
Mishnah (oral law) and the Gemara (commentary and
analysis of the Mishnah).

Tanakh

The Hebrew Bible, comprising three main parts: Torah (Law), Nevi'im (Prophets), and Ketuvim (Writings).

Torah
The central and most sacred text of Judaism, comprising the first five books of the Hebrew Bible, also known as the Pentateuch.

Yom Kippur
The Jewish Day of Atonement, observed with fasting and prayers, focusing on repentance and forgiveness.

ABOUT THE AUTHOR

 Alex is an armchair historian, developing an early interest in military history from stories told by his Grandfathers and even his Great-Grandfather, who fought at the Somme.

He also has a keen interest and understanding of ancient history, military leaders throughout history, religion and philosophy. Through his books, Alex hopes to spark a healthy curiosity and love for history in his readers.

When not working or spending time with his wife, Beverley, and children, Rory and Lucy, Alex can be found walking his two black Labradors in the local countryside, pondering ideas for his next book.

Printed in Great Britain
by Amazon

32457922R00066